SUPERHUMAN STRENGTH

Kelly Doudna

Big Buddy Books
An Imprint of Abdo Publishing
abdobooks.com

abdobooks.com

Published by Abdo Publishing, a division of ABDO, PO Box 398166, Minneapolis, Minnesota 55439.

Printed in the United States of America, North Mankato, Minnesota
102021
012022

THIS BOOK CONTAINS RECYCLED MATERIALS

Design: Emily O'Malley, Mighty Media, Inc.
Production: Mighty Media, Inc.
Editor: Rebecca Felix
Cover Photographs: Shutterstock Images
Interior Photographs: Courtesy of 360Films, p. 25; iStockphoto, p. 21; MediaNews Group/Orange County Register/Getty Images, p. 23; Paula R. Lively/Wikimedia Commons, p. 15; Shutterstock Images, pp. 5, 7, 9, 11 (top, bottom), 13, 17, 19, 27, 28, 29
Design Elements: Shutterstock Images

Library of Congress Control Number: 2021942809

Publisher's Cataloging-in-Publication Data
Names: Doudna, Kelly, author.
Title: Superhuman strength / by Kelly Doudna
Description: Minneapolis, Minnesota : Abdo Publishing, 2022 | Series: Superhuman science | Includes online resources and index.
Identifiers: ISBN 9781532197048 (lib. bdg.) | ISBN 9781644947203 (pbk.) | ISBN 9781098219178 (ebook)
Subjects: LCSH: Human physiology--Juvenile literature. | Performance--Juvenile literature. | Motor ability--Juvenile literature. | Muscle strength--Juvenile literature. | Super powers--Juvenile literature.
Classification: DDC 599.9--dc23

DON'T TRY THIS AT HOME

Many of the superhuman feats described in this book were overseen by trainers and doctors. Do not attempt to re-create these feats. Doing so could cause injury.

CONTENTS

AMAZING ABILITY

Superheroes have superpowers. But real men and women also have **amazing** abilities. Some people have superhuman strength!

Athletes flip huge tires in the 2011 Strongman Champions League in Spain to determine who is the strongest.

WHAT IS STRENGTH?

Strength is the ability to produce force. Force is a push or pull that makes something move or change shape. The stronger you are, the more force you can produce.

PUSH & PULL

Tons of daily actions use force! For example, you pull a door open and push it shut.

A weak kick produces less force.

A strong kick produces more force.

MIGHTY MUSCLES

Human strength comes from muscles. Some muscles connect bones. When you move a muscle, the bones connected to it also move.

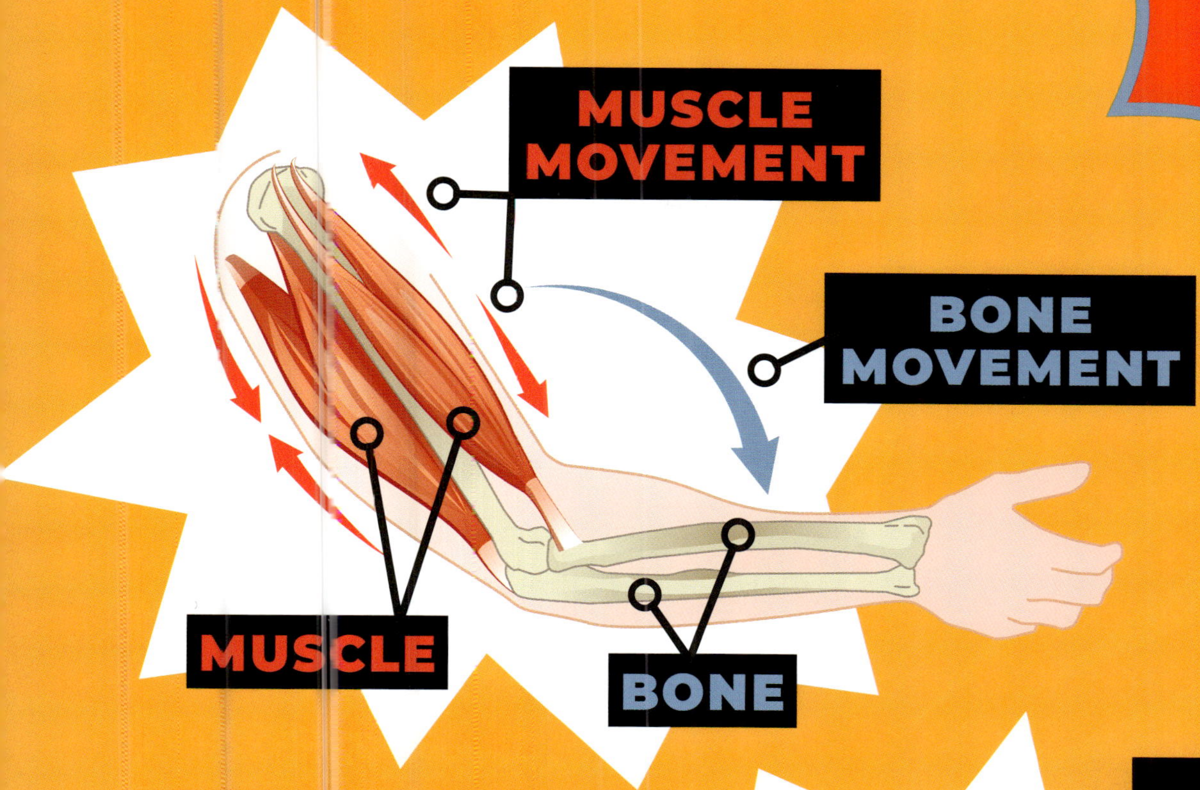
MUSCLE
MOVEMENT
BONE
MOVEMENT
MUSCLE
BONE

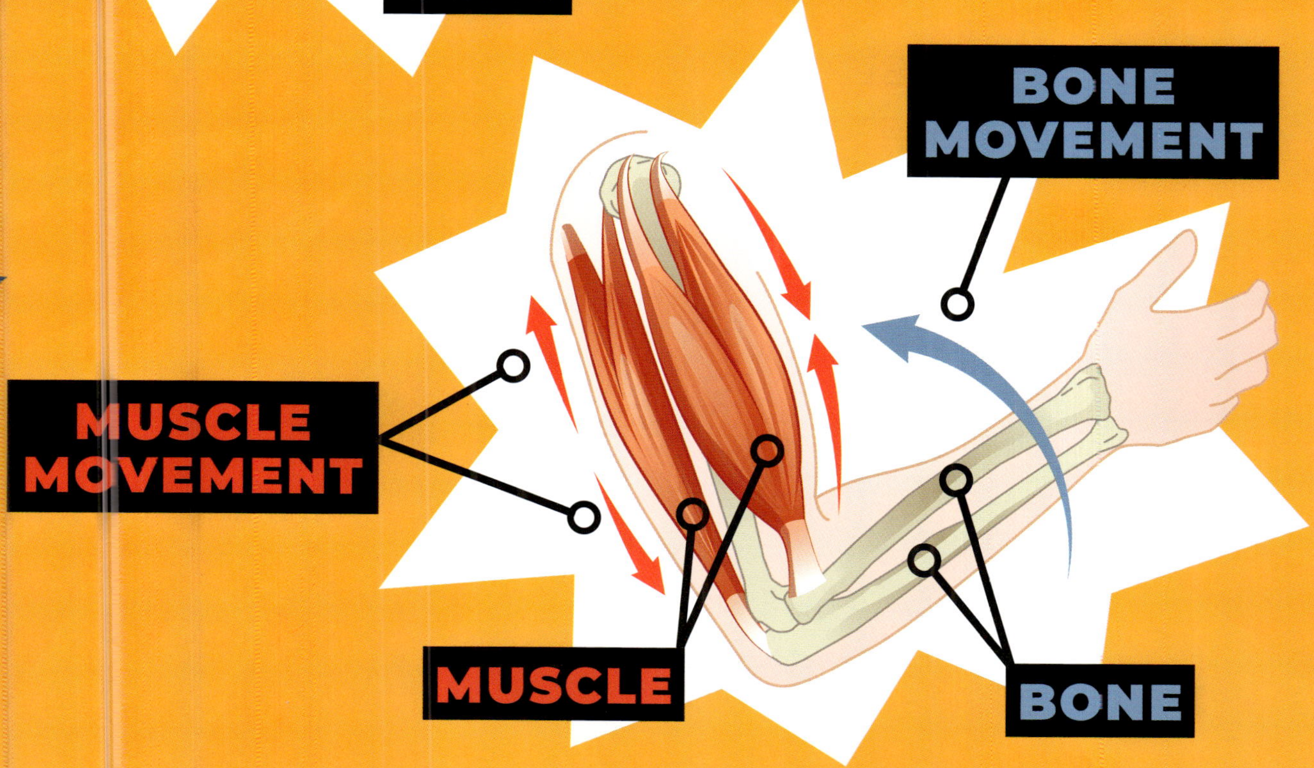
BONE
MOVEMENT
MUSCLE
MOVEMENT
MUSCLE
BONE

BUILDING MUSCLE

Everyone is born with muscles. But some people work hard to make their muscles stronger.

Weight training is one way to strengthen muscles.

BIGGER & STRONGER

Professional weightlifters use special workouts to strengthen their muscles. They learn safe **techniques**. So, they are less likely to get hurt.

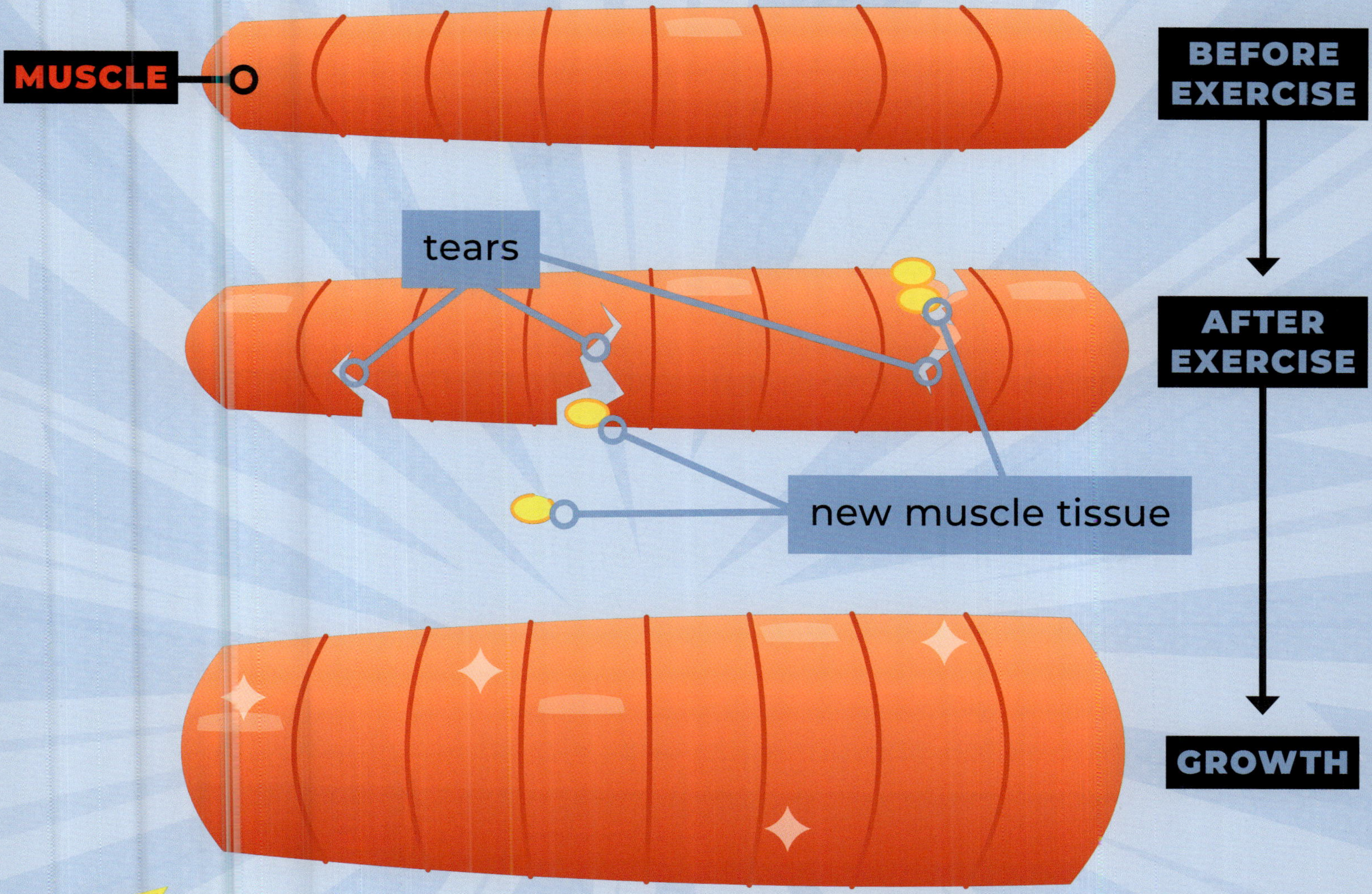

Your muscles tear a little bit during resistance training, or weightlifting. New muscle tissue grows to heal the tears. This makes the muscles bigger and stronger.

Professional American weightlifter Brian Shaw has won several strongman **competitions**. One event he performs is the harness pull. Shaw can pull an airplane! He uses a harness, a rope, and his superhuman strength.

At the 2017 Arnold Strongman Classic competition, Brian Shaw lifted 991 pounds (450 kg)!

FIGHT OR FLIGHT

Some people get bursts of strength outside their normal abilities. They experience fight-or-flight responses in **emergencies**. This response gets their body ready for action.

FIGHT-OR-FLIGHT REACTIONS

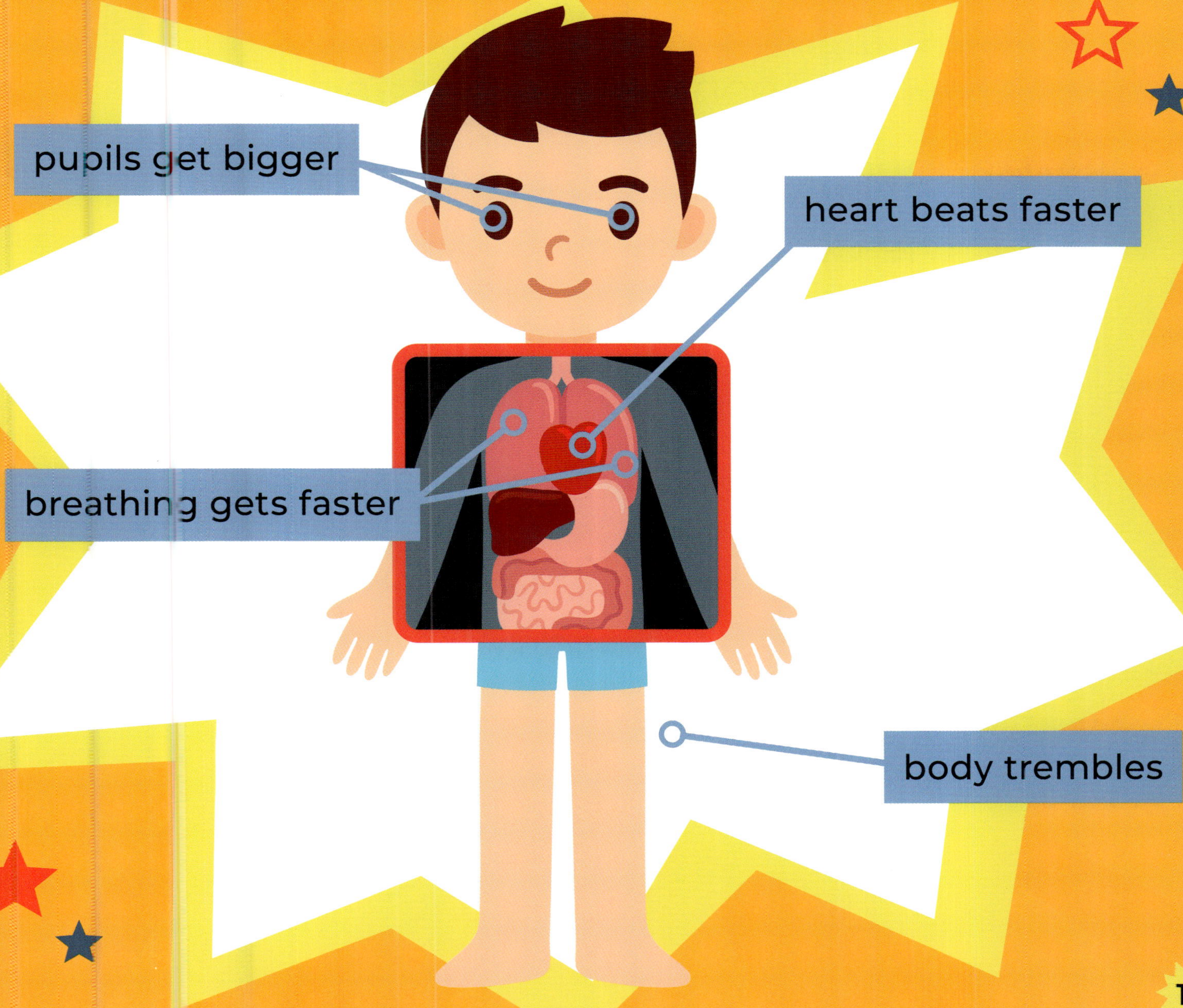

In 2006, Tom Boyle saw a cyclist who had been hit by a car and was trapped under it. Boyle lifted the car off the cyclist!

Boyle was a weightlifter. But the car weighed much more than he had ever lifted. Boyle's body had a fight response to the **emergency**. This helped him have more strength and feel less pain when lifting the car.

A Chevrolet Camaro can weigh more than 4,000 pounds (1,814 kg)! Tom Boyle raised the car's front end. The car's driver pulled the cyclist out from under the car.

FEEL THE BURN

Muscles use oxygen. When you repeat a movement over and over, your body can't send enough oxygen to your muscles. Instead, your body makes **lactate**.

Lactate gives your muscles an energy boost. But lactic acid builds up in the muscles. This causes a burning **sensation**.

The burn from lactic acid is your body telling you to rest. This helps prevent permanent harm to your muscles.

Well-trained weightlifters can move huge amounts of weight. But lactic acid still affects them. So, **repetition** events usually only last for about one minute.

Liefia Ingalls is an American champion strongwoman. She performs fast repetitions with heavy objects. She has lifted 500 pounds (226 kg) 6 times in about 30 seconds!

Liefia Ingalls won the women's division at the 2016 California Strongest Man Competition.

SUPER SQUEEZE

Another way to show strength is **squeezing**. Squeezing puts force on opposite sides of an object.

American Kortney Olson has **incredibly** strong thighs. She has recorded herself crushing watermelons with them!

Kortney Olson squeezes a watermelon between her thighs. She has said she hopes her feats inspire others to be stronger.

Olson also appeared on the TV show *Stan Lee's Superhumans* along with a python. There, a researcher used **sensors** to compare Olson's and the snake's **squeeze** forces. Olson's thighs produced a greater force than the python!

DEATH SQUEEZE

A python is a constrictor. It wraps around its prey and squeezes it to death.

Some pythons can squeeze at 80 pounds per square inch (5.6 kg/cm^2) and hold it for 10 minutes!

STRONG FINISH

Want to increase your strength? Try doing arm curls!

1. Fill a 32-ounce (1 L) bottle with water.
2. Hold the bottle in your hand with your palm facing up.

3. Bend your elbow to bring the bottle toward your shoulder. Straighten your arm. Repeat until your arm is tired.
4. Repeat steps 2 and 3 with your other arm.

Do this exercise a few times a week. Soon you'll be able to do more **repetitions** or use a heavier bottle!

GLOSSARY

amazing—causing wonder or surprise.

competition (kahm-puh-TIH-shuhn)—a contest between two or more persons or groups.

emergency (ih-MUHR-juhnt-see)—an unexpected event that requires immediate action.

incredibly—in a way that is amazing or unbelievable.

lactate—a compound of lactic acid.

repetition—the act of repeating or being repeated.

sensation—a physical feeling.

sensor—an instrument that can detect, measure, and transmit information to a controlling device.

squeeze—to tightly press the sides of something together.

technique (tehk-NEEK)—a method or style in which something is done.

ONLINE RESOURCES

Booklinks
NONFICTION NETWORK
FREE! ONLINE NONFICTION RESOURCES

To learn more about superhuman strength, please visit **abdobooklinks.com** or scan this QR code. These links are routinely monitored and updated to provide the most current information available.

INDEX